To the Depths of the Ocean

Rod Theodorou

Heinemann Library
Chicago, Illinois

©2000 Reed Educational & Professional Publishing
Published by Heinemann Library,
an imprint of Reed Educational & Professional Publishing,
Chicago, IL

Customer Service 888-454-2279

Visit our website at www.heinemannlibrary.com

Designed by AMR

Printed in China

05 04
10 9 8 7 6 5 4

Library of Congress Cataloging-in-Publication Data
Theodorou, Rod.
        To the depths of the ocean / Rod Theodorou.
            p. cm. – (Amazing journeys)
        Includes bibliographical references and index.
        ISBN 1-57572-484-7 (library binding)   ISBN 1-58810-306-4 (paperback binding)
        1. Oceanography Juvenile literature. 2. Ocean—Juvenile
literature. I. Title. II. Series: Theodorou, Rod.
        Amazing journeys.
        GC21.5.T48 2000
        551.46—dc21   99-37169
                                                CIP

Acknowledgments
The Publishers would like to thank the following for permission to reproduce photographs:
BBC/Jeff Rotman, p. 16; NHPA/Norbert Wu, pp. 10, 21, 23; Oxford Scientific Films/David B Fleetman, p.15; Oxford Scientific Films/Doug Allan, p. 23; Oxford Scientific Films/Gerard Soury, p .18; Howard Hall, pp. 11, 13, 19; Oxford Scientific Films/Kathie Atkinson, p. 11; Oxford Scientific Films/Ken Smith Laboratory/Scripps, p. 25; Oxford Scientific Films/Liz Bomford, p. 27; Oxford Scientific Films/Norbert Wu, pp. 17, 21; Oxford Scientific Films/Paul Kay, p. 23; Oxford Scientific Films/Peter Parks, pp. 13, 20; Oxford Scientific Films/Steve Early, p. 15; Science Photo Library/NASA, p. 6; Science Photo Library/Peter Ryan/Scripps, p. 24.

Cover photograph reproduced with permission of Bruce Coleman Collection.

Every effort has been made to contact copyright holders of any material reproduced in this book. Any omissions will be rectified in subsequent printings if notice is given to the Publisher.

Some words are shown in bold, **like this.**
You can find out what they mean by looking in the glossary.

Contents

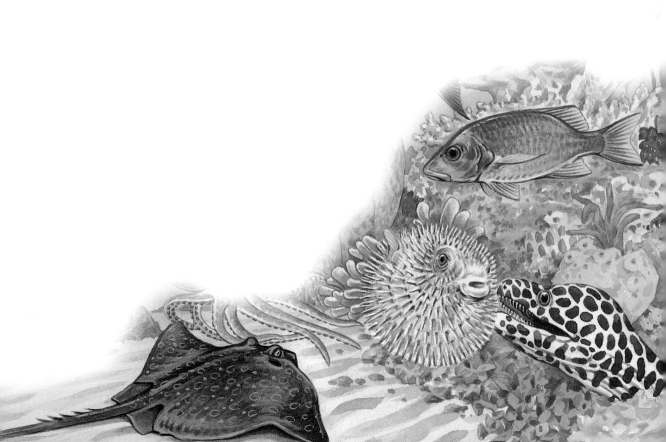

Introduction

You are about to go on an amazing journey. You are going to climb inside a **submersible**, an advanced small submarine, and be lowered off a ship into the swelling waters of the Pacific Ocean. Millions of animals live beneath the waves, each one specially adapted to survive in this hostile environment.

You will begin your journey among glittering silver **schools** of fish, pursued by fast lone hunters. Then you are going to descend into the gloomy depths to view an amazing alien environment. You will see incredible creatures, huge **predators**, and animals unknown to science until very recently.

With the help of a submersible like this, you are about to explore the depths of the mighty Pacific Ocean.

Viewed from space, Earth looks like a blue planet. Over 70 percent of its surface is covered by seawater. The oceans are the most unexplored places on Earth. Most are over 13,123 feet (4,000 meters) deep. Only the first 650 feet (about 200 meters) of this water is warm and lit by the sun. The rest is dark and cold, but it is not lifeless.

Some parts of the ocean are incredibly deep. Arizona's Grand Canyon is a spectacular, deep land **gorge** over 5,250 feet (1,600 meters) deep. But compare this to the deepest part of the Pacific Ocean—the Marianas Trench is more than 36,200 feet (11,000 meters) deep! What kind of creatures could survive in such pitch-black, freezing depths?

The submersible's hatch is closing. You are about to find out.

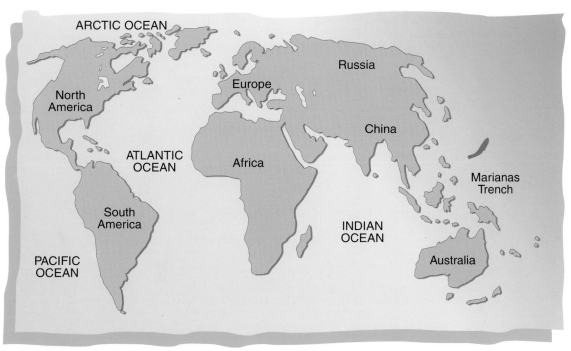

The world's oceans

Journey Map

Page 10

Page 12

near shore zone

Page 14

continental shelf

continental slope

Page 16

Here is a map of our undersea journey. You can see that each part of the ocean has a name. We start in shallow waters and move away from the coast, going deeper as we go. This is called the sunlit zone. We will come to the edge of the **continental shelf** and drop down into the deep open ocean. The sunlight cannot shine deeper than about 650 feet (200 meters). The gloomy waters below are called the twilight zone. By the time we reach the 3,200-feet (1,000-meter) mark, it will be completely black outside the **porthole** window. We will need to turn on our submersible's lights to see any life as we sink farther down toward the very bottom of the ocean.

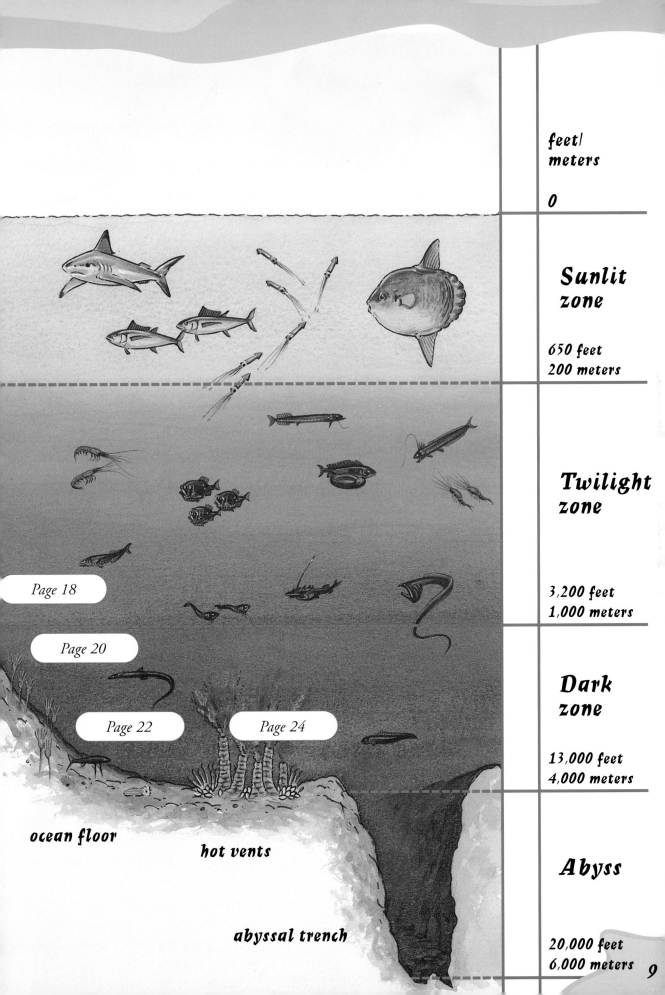

feet/
meters

0

Sunlit
zone

650 feet
200 meters

Twilight
zone

Page 18

3,200 feet
1,000 meters

Page 20

Dark
zone

Page 22   Page 24

13,000 feet
4,000 meters

ocean floor

hot vents

Abyss

abyssal trench

20,000 feet
6,000 meters

At the Surface

As the **submersible** is lowered over the side of our ship, we have one last look at the sky and waves. Gulls and a lone albatross soar overhead. We are lucky enough to see a huge manta ray, frightened by some undersea **predator**, leap out of the water. Tiny flying fish also break the surface and glide above the wave crests before disappearing again. With a loud thud, the submersible smacks into the sea, and, in a burst of bubbles, we sink beneath the surface. The dolphins that have been following our ship soon come to investigate. Bright sunlight glints off the silver fish that pass by in large **schools**. There is life all around us.

The "wings" of a huge manta ray break the surface of the water.

Portuguese man-of-war

Each Portuguese man-of-war is actually a **colony** of smaller animals that live together. One is a large gas-filled float that sticks up above the surface and acts like a sail, moving the colony along. Others are stinging **tentacles** that catch food.

Sailfish

This fast hunter has a streamlined body built for speed. It can swim at an amazing 68 miles (109 km) per hour, faster than a cheetah can run!

Flying fish

A flying fish being chased by a predator gathers speed and then jumps out of the water. It spreads out its large fins, which act like wings, carrying the flying fish through the air for about 30 seconds.

The Teeming Shallows

Many of the fish we see in the sunlit zone are dark green-blue on the top and silver underneath. This coloring makes it hard for them to be seen by **predators** from above (looking downward at the green-blue depths) or below (looking up at the silvery surface).

Invisible to our eyes are millions of tiny **plankton**. In spring and summer, they multiply in vast numbers. The plant-plankton grow in the warm sunlight, and the animal-plankton feed on them. They also feed on other tiny food **particles** that are carried toward the ocean's surface by storms or undersea **currents**. Smaller fish feast on this plankton. Larger fish eat the smaller fish. Even giant whales eat plankton, plus other tiny shrimps called krill. Without plankton, most other ocean life would die.

1. ocean sunfish
2. skipjack tuna
3. manta ray
4. Pacific sardine
5. common dolphin
6. blue shark
7. cod
8. dolphin fish
9. krill
10. Pacific right whale
11. basking shark

The shallow water is lit up by the sun's rays and is full of life.

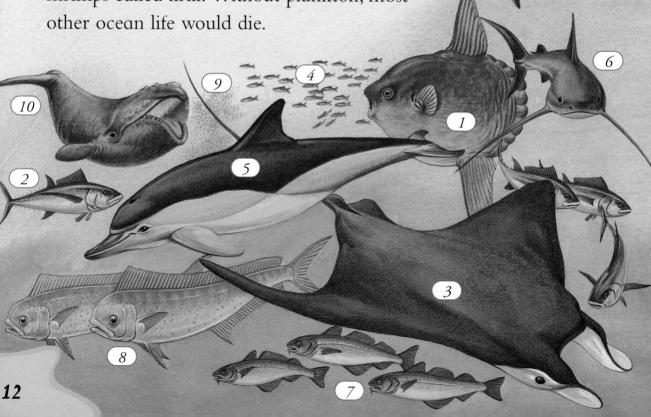

Plankton

Plankton are microscopic creatures. Some are tiny plants. Others are tiny animals that eat the plant-plankton. Some are fish **fry** or the tiny **larvae** of other sea animals.

Whale shark

At 60 feet (18 meters) long, this is the largest fish in the world. It is completely harmless and wanders the ocean alone, feeding on plankton.

Pacific salmon

Salmon hatch in freshwater streams and then **migrate** to the sea. They live in the ocean for several years before traveling huge distances back to the same streams where they hatched. There they **spawn** and then die.

The Continental Shelf

The **submersible** dives deeper. We can't see the ocean surface any more, but the temperature **gauge** indicates the water is still warm, about 50°F (15 °C), and there is still a lot of light. We catch sight of the seabed below us. We are now at the **continental shelf**.

The submersible's whining **propeller** blades slow down for a while as we stop to enjoy the life around us. A green turtle flaps slowly by on its way to feed on turtle grass, a kind of seaweed. Before us we can see the edge of the continental shelf. Soon we will have to go over that cliff edge and drop down the steep continental slope into deeper, darker waters.

The continental shelf marks the end of the shallows and the beginning of deep water.

1. coral
2. sponges
3. seaweed
4. green turtle
5. barracuda
6. jellyfish
7. hammerhead shark
8. red snapper
9. California sea-lion
10. spotted eagle ray
11. Pacific octopus
12. puffer fish
13. moray eel

Blue spotted ray

Like most rays, it spends much of its life on the seabed where it is hard for **predators** to spot. If attacked, it can defend itself with the two **venomous spines** in its tail.

Pacific lobster

This brightly colored **scavenger** hides among rocks during the day. At night, it comes out to feed on worms and other small animals.

Pacific octopus

This giant octopus can grow much bigger than a human! Its arms can span 30 feet (9 meters), but it is a very shy and gentle animal. Its favorite foods are crabs and lobsters.

The Twilight Zone

*A*s we dive farther down the continental slope, things start to change. It gets much colder—the temperature **gauge** drops to 41° F (5 °C). We are so deep we can see hardly any sunlight. We switch on the **submersible's** lights.

There are far fewer fish down here, but our lights soon attract them. The deeper we go, the stranger the fish look. Many of the fish and shrimp here have what look like tiny headlights. These are special **organs** on their skin that produce light. The light is used to identify and attract a **mate** or to attract **prey**. Some animals can "turn on" these lights in a sudden flash of brilliance to confuse a **predator**.

These squid have large eyes to help them see in the darkness, and light organs to help them be seen.

Hatchet fish

Most hunters in the twilight zone look upward to see if they can spot the dark shadow of another fish against the dim light above them. Hatchet fish have light organs along their bellies and tails that make them glow just enough to match the light above them. Viewed from below, these fish are almost invisible to predators. Like many fish in the twilight zone, they swim upward at night, when many predators are asleep, to feed in the richer, shallower waters.

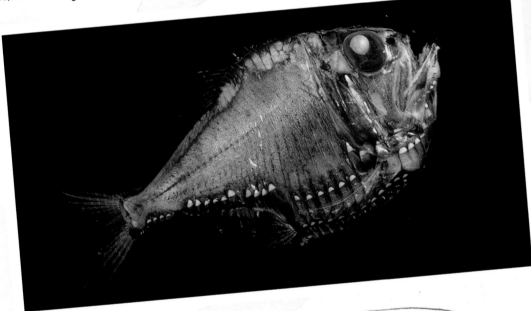

Viper fish

Like many twilight hunters, these fish have huge jaws filled with large fangs and a special fin with a light on the end. This **lure** acts like a fishing rod, attracting smaller prey, which the viper fish gobbles up.

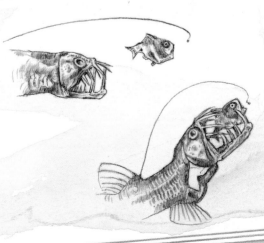

Deep-Water Giants

We have been traveling down for over two hours now. Below 650 feet (200 meters) there is so little light that no plant life can grow. Therefore there is no **plankton** down here. The fish feed on dead **carcasses** or droppings that fall down from above, or on each other.

Suddenly we pick up something huge on our **radar**. Two sperm whales are diving straight down into the depths to feed. We peer out the **porthole**. These incredible whales are shaped like submarines and can dive to amazing depths to hunt for their favorite **prey**, giant squid.

Sperm whales have tiny eyes but can find their prey in the darkness using **sonar**.

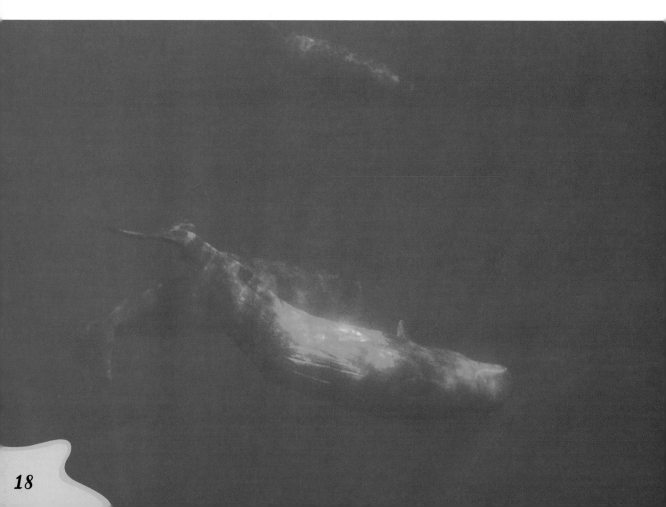

Whipnose

The whipnose uses its incredibly long **lure** to attract prey into coming closer to its hungry mouth.

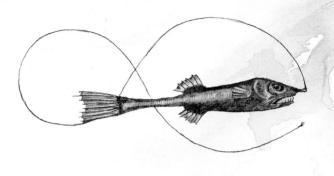

Sperm whale

The huge, blunt **snout** of the sperm whale acts like a heavy weight, helping it sink down quickly into the depths to hunt. The whale can hold its breath for over an hour!

Giant squid

These massive, mysterious animals can weigh over 2,000 pounds (907 kilograms) and may be longer than the whales that hunt them. The dead bodies of giant squid have washed onto beaches, but they have never been filmed alive.

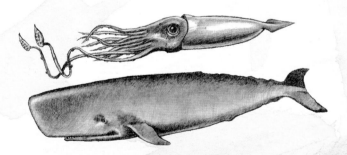

Into the Darkness

We are very deep now — deeper than 3,200 feet (1,000 meters). The immense weight of the water above us presses down on the **titanium hull** of our **submersible**. This **pressure** would crush a diver like a paper cup. The water is nearly freezing, and there's no light. When we switch off the submersible's lights and look through the thick **porthole,** all we see is inky blackness. Down in this alien world, many of the animals are completely blind. They are often colored black, making them hard to see even with our lights back on. There is very little food down here. **Predators** will attack and try to gobble up any fish they find, no matter what the size.

Many deep-sea fish, like this dragonfish, have a long thread called a **lure,** which they use like a fishing rod to attract their **prey**.

Fangtooth

The fangtooth's mouth bristles with huge teeth. This fish is also called an ogrefish—for obvious reasons!

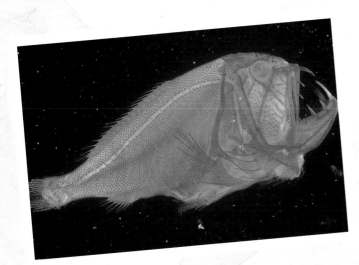

Gulper eel

The gulper eel is like a giant swimming mouth. It drifts along until it meets another fish, then it opens its huge mouth and strikes.

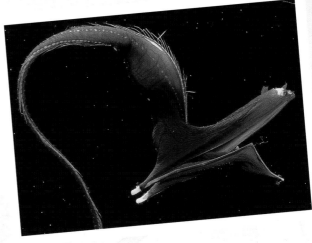

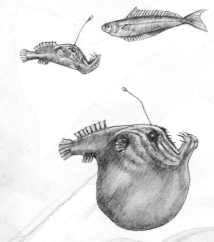

Deep-sea angler

The female angler fish grows to 3 feet (1 meter) long, but the male is tiny. The male spends its life holding onto the female. She has a lure tipped with a light organ and a huge baglike stomach, which can hold fish up to twice her own size!

At the Ocean Floor

We are nearly 10,000 feet (3,000 meters) down now. The **hull** of the **submersible** creaks and groans under the enormous **pressure** above. The water outside is below freezing. Suddenly our lights reveal the ocean floor just below us.

The surface of the ocean floor is made up of the tiny skeletons and droppings of millions of animals. This mixture forms a thick layer of mud that stirs up into a cloud if touched. It is like a desert here. There is not even any seaweed. As we move along above the mud, we start to see more snails and worms making their way slowly and carefully along the muddy ooze.

1. deep-sea prawn
2. sea cucumber
3. nudibranch
4. sea urchin
5. sea lilies
6. rat fish
7. halosaur
8. tripod fish
9. brittle star

The floor of the deep ocean is a still, barren desert.

Tripod fish

The special fins of this fish help it to "stand" above the ocean floor and wait to catch the **scent** of any food nearby.

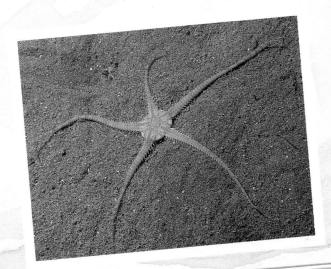

Sea spider

This strange blind creature is not a real spider, though it is related to spiders. It walks along the seabed on its spindly legs, trying to find worms to eat.

Brittle star

These delicate starfish feed on tiny food **particles** they find on the seabed. If an attacker bites off one of the arms of a brittle star, it can grow another.

The Hot Vents

Suddenly our temperature **gauge** starts to rise. How can we be in warmer water? We notice more fish. Then we discover the reason. Deep below us, water is being heated by hot **lava** that shoots up through cracks in the ocean floor. **Minerals** from the lava are being deposited on the seabed in tall **vents** like chimneys. The water is also full of **sulfur**, which is eaten by **bacteria**. A whole **colony** of amazing animals lives around each chimney, feeding on the bacteria.

Beyond us is another cliff edge leading to a deep-water trench. We cannot go any deeper. It is time to return to the surface. Who knows what creatures remain to be discovered in this amazing and wonderful world?

Huge worms and clams feed on the mineral-eating bacteria at ocean-floor vents. Fish, crabs, shrimp, and anemones also live around the vents.

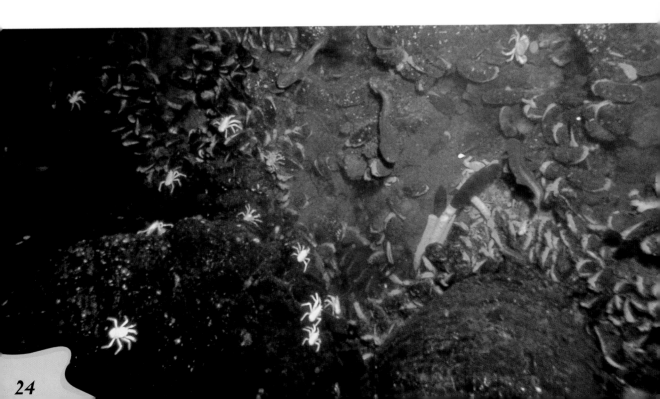

Tube worms

Huge red worms in long white tubes live around the chimneys. They grow up to 3 feet (1 meter) long.

A special world

Until these vents were discovered, it was thought that all life on the planet needed the sun to survive. Plants cannot grow without sunlight. Without plants, every other life form would die. The amazing thing about hot vents is that the animals around them do not need sunlight to stay alive.

Large clams

Large white clams that can reach 12 inches (30 cm) in length also live and feed around the vents.

Conservation and the Future

Pollution

People have always treated the ocean like a huge sewer. It was thought that the seas were so big and so deep that anything could be thrown into them and it would be washed away. Sewage, garbage, and industrial waste such as petroleum and chemical poisons were dumped straight into the sea. Scientists have recently realized that **pollutants** do enormous damage in the sea. Many chemicals are eaten by tiny sea creatures, which are then eaten by fish—and finally by people!

Many countries now have laws to control and stop ocean polluting, but a huge amount of sea dumping still occurs.

Although it is illegal, Captains of oil tankers still dump huge amounts of unwanted oil into the sea, killing thousands of sea birds.

Over-fishing

Many fish and other animals have been hunted by humans almost to **extinction**. Modern fishing boats have **sonar** that locates fish, as well as huge nets to catch whole **schools** at one time. Larger animals, such as dolphins and sharks, are often caught in these nets by accident and die. Many countries are trying to control over-fishing. Most whale hunting has been banned, but it may be too late for some species, such as the white beluga whale.

One new idea is to protect special areas of the sea where no one can pollute or kill the wildlife. These nature reserves are helping to preserve **marine** wildlife for the future.

The largest protected marine area is the Great Barrier Reef Marine Park off the coast of Australia.

Glossary

bacteria	tiny organisms that live in the soil, in water, and in the bodies of animals and plants and that can be helpful or harmful
carcass	dead body (usually of an animal)
colony	group of similar things living together
continental shelf	gradually sloping shallow area of seabed between the land and the depths of the water
current	movement of water, sometimes caused by the tide
extinction	permanent disappearance of a type of animal or plant
fry	young fish
gauge	instrument for measuring or testing something
gorge	very deep, steep-sided valley cut into the ground by a river
hull	body of a boat or ship
larva	(More than one are called **larvae**) insect or other animal after it has changed from an egg but is not yet an adult
lava	hot, melting rock that oozes from cracks in the earth
lure	organ that lights up on a fish's head to attract prey
marine	to do with the sea
mate	of a male and a female, to join to produce babies
migrate	to move from one place to another, often to feed or mate
mineral	natural substance found in the earth, such as coal or gold
organ	part of a body that does a specific job to make the body work
particle	very small amount of something

plankton	tiny animal and plant life that floats or swims in water
pollutant	anything that makes air, water, or land dirty
porthole	window in the side of a ship
predator	animal that hunts, kills, and eats other animals
pressure	weight of something pressing or being pressed
prey	animal that serves as food for other animals
propeller	blade that turns quickly to help a vehicle move through water or air
radar	way of finding things by reflecting radio waves from them
scavenger	animal that looks for and feeds on leftovers or dead animals
scent	smell
school	large group of the same type of fish
snout	animal's nose and mouth when they are together
sonar	(SOund and NAvigation Ranging) way of finding objects, especially underwater, using reflected sound waves
spawn	to lay large numbers of eggs
spine	special stiff or pointed fish fin
submersible	underwater craft used for deep-sea research
sulfur	chemical element similar to oxygen (also spelled sulphur)
tentacle	long and flexible part of some animals that is used to feel and touch
titanium	silver-gray, light but very strong, metal
venomous	poisonous
vent	opening through which a gas or liquid can escape

More Books to Read

Clarke, Penny. *Beneath the Oceans.* New York: Franklin Watts, Inc. 1997.

Dipper, Francis. *The Ocean Deep.* Danbury, Conn.: Millbrook Press, Inc., 1996.

Morris, Neil. *Oceans & Seas.* Austin, Tex.: Raintree Steck-Vaughn, 1997.

Oldershaw, Callie. *Oceans.* Troll Communications L.L.C., 1997.

Savage, Stephen. *Animals of the Oceans.* Austin, Tex.: Raintree Steck-Vaughn, 1997.

Talbot, Frank H. *Under the Sea.* Alexandria, Va.: Time-Life, Inc., 1995.

Telford, Carole, and Rod Theodorou. *Inside a Coral Reef.* Des Plaines, Ill: Heinemann Library, 1998.

—.*Shark and Dolphin.* Des Plaines, Ill.: Heinemann Library, 1997.

Wroble, Lisa A. *The Oceans.* San Diego:Lucent Books, 1998.

Organizations

Cousteau Society
870 Greenbrier Circle
Suite 402
Chesapeake, Va. 23320
Tel. (800) 441-4395

Earthwatch Institute U.S.
680 Mount Auburn Street
Watertown, Mass. 02471
Tel. (800) 776-0188

Greenpeace U.S.A.
1436 U Street N.W
Washington, D.C. 20009
Tel. (202) 462-1177

National Wildlife Federation
8925 Leesburg Pike
Vienna, Va. 22184
Tel. (703) 790-4100

Save the Whales
PO Box 2397
Venice, CA 90291

Index